GOSCINNY AND UDERZO
PRESENT
AN ASTERIX ADVENTURE

ASTERIX AND THE SECRET WEAPON

WRITTEN AND ILLUSTRATED BY ALBERT UDERZO
TRANSLATED BY ANTHEA BELL AND DEREK HOCKRIDGE

D0308497

HODDER AND STOUGHTON
LONDON SYDNEY AUCKLAND

ASTERIX IN OTHER COUNTRIES

Australia	Hodder Dargaud, Rydalmere Business Park, 10/16 South Street, Rydalmere, N.S.W. 2116, Australia
Austria	Delta Verlag, Postfach 10 12 45, 7000 Stuttgart 1, Germany
Belgium	Dargaud Bénélux, 3 rue Kindermans, 1050 Brussels, Belgium
Brazil	Record Distribuidora, Rua Argentina 171, 20921 Rio de Janeiro, Brazil
Canada	*(French)* Dargaud Canada, Presse-Import, 307 Benjamin Hudon, St Laurent, Montreal, Quebec H4N 1J1, Canada
	(English) General Publishing Co. Ltd, 30 Lesmill Road, Don Mills, Ontario M38 2T6, Canada
Denmark	Serieforlaget A/S (Gutenberghus Group), Vognmagergade 11, 1148 Copenhagen K, Denmark
Finland	Sanoma Corporation, P.O. Box 107, 00381 Helsinki 38, Finland
France	Dargaud Editeur, 6 Rue Gager-Gabillot, 75015 Paris, France
	(titles up to and including Asterix in Belgium)
	Les Editions Albert René, 26 Avenue Victor Hugo, 75116 Paris, France
	(titles from Asterix and the Great Divide onwards)
Germany	Delta Verlag, Postfach 10 12 45, 7000 Stuttgart 1, Germany
Greece	Mamouth Comix Ltd, Ippokratous 57, 106080 Athens, Greece
Holland	Dargaud Bénélux, 3 rue Kindermans, 1050 Brussels, Belgium
	(Distribution) Betapress, Burg. Krollaan 14, 5126 PT, Jilze, Holland
Hong Kong	Hodder Dargaud, c/o Publishers Associates Ltd, 11th Floor, Taikoo Trading Estate, 28 Tong Cheong Street, Quarry Bay, Hong Kong
Hungary	Egmont Pannonia, Pannonhalmi ut. 14, 1118 Budapest, Hungary
Indonesia	Penerbit Sinar Harapan, J1. Dewi Sartika 136D, Jakarta Cawang, Indonesia
Italy	Mondadori, Via Belvedere, 37131 Verona, Italy
Latin America	Grijalbo-Dargaud S.A., Aragon 385, 08013 Barcelona, Spain
Luxemburg	Imprimerie St. Paul, rue Christophe Plantin 2, Luxemburg
New Zealand	Hodder Dargaud, P.O. Box 3858, Auckland 1, New Zealand
Norway	A/S Hjemmet (Gutenburghus Group), Kristian den 4des gt. 13, Oslo 1, Norway
Portugal	Meriberica-Liber, Avenida Duque d'Avila 69, R/C esq., 1000 Lisbon, Portugal
Roman Empire	*(Latin)* Delta Verlag, Postfach 10 12 45, 7000 Stuttgart 1, Germany
Southern Africa	Hodder Dargaud, c/o Struik Book Distributors (Pty) Ltd, Graph Avenue, Montague Gardens 7441, South Africa
Spain	Grijalbo-Dargaud S.A., Aragon 385, 08013 Barcelona, Spain
Sweden	Hemmets Journal (Gutenghus Group), Fack, 200 22 Malmö, Sweden
Switzerland	Dargaud (Suisse) S.A., En Budron B, 1052 Le Mont sur Lausanne, Switzerland
Wales	*(Welsh)* Gwasg Y Dref Wen, 28 Church Road, Whitchurch, Cardiff, Wales
Yugoslavia	Nip Forum, Vojvode Misica 1-3, 2100 Novi Sad, Yugoslavia

British Library Cataloguing in Publication Data

A catalogue record for this book is available from the British Library

ISBN 0 340 56295 1 (cased)
ISBN 0 340 56871 2 (limp)

Original edition © Les Editions Albert René, Goscinny-Uderzo, 1991
English translation © Les Editions Albert René, Goscinny-Uderzo, 1991
Exclusive licensee: Hodder and Stoughton Ltd
Translators: Anthea Bell and Derek Hockridge
Hand-lettering: Stephen Potter

First published in Great Britain 1991 (cased)
This impression 92 93 94 95 96

First published in Great Britain 1993 (limp)

Published by Hodder Dargaud Ltd,
Mill Road, Dunton Green, Sevenoaks, Kent TN13 2YA

Printed in Belgium by Proost International Book Production

GOSCINNYRIX · VDERZORIX

VIS COMICA *

* The power to make people laugh: from an epigram by Caesar on Terence, the Latin poet.

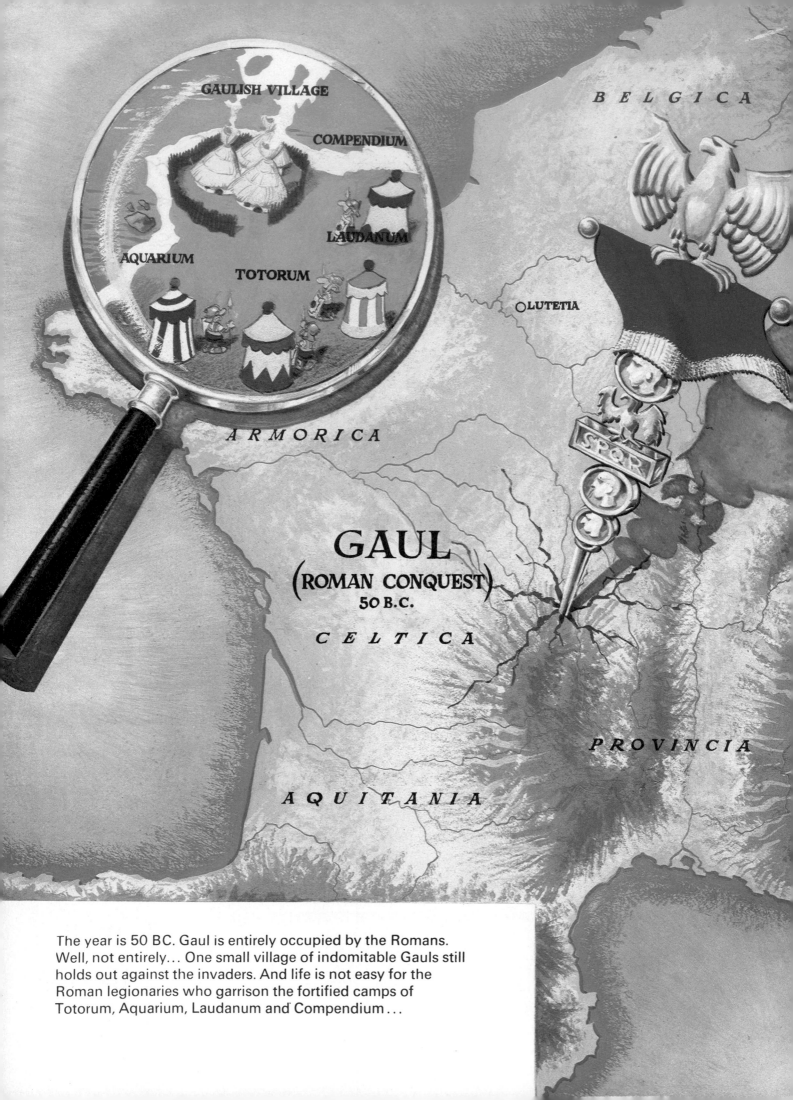

The year is 50 BC. Gaul is entirely occupied by the Romans. Well, not entirely... One small village of indomitable Gauls still holds out against the invaders. And life is not easy for the Roman legionaries who garrison the fortified camps of Totorum, Aquarium, Laudanum and Compendium...

COME ALONG, CHILDREN! BREAK'S OVER!

BONG! BONG! BONG!

WE'VE DECIDED TO REMOVE OUR CHILDREN FROM THIS SCHOOL! IT HAS A POOR REPUTATION!

?!?

SCHOOL

WHAT'S MORE, WE'VE APPOINTED A NEW TEACHER FROM LUTETIA! SHE'S GOING TO SEE TO THEIR EDUCATION!

SPECIALLY THEIR **MUSICAL** EDUCATION!

!

ALLOW ME TO REMIND YOU THAT ONLY DRUIDS AND BARDS ARE QUALIFIED TO TEACH SCHOOLCHILDREN!

OH, SO A WOMAN CAN'T BE A BARD?

NO, MA'AM! SHE'S BARRED FROM BEING A BARD!!!

THAT'S JUST TOO BARD! TAKE THAT!

KEEP YOUR HANDS TO YOURSELF, MA'AM!

PAFF!

NO HOLDS BARRED, EH?

NOT ONLY DO THEY THUMP ME AT THE DROP OF A LYRE, THEY'RE BRINGING IN A FOREIGN FEMALE TO REPLACE ME! WELL, THAT'S IT! I'M LEAVING THE VILLAGE!

POOR OLD CACOFONIX! HE REALLY SEEMS TO MEAN IT! I'D BETTER GO AND TELL CHIEF VITALSTATISTIX!

IT'S NO SKIN OFF MY NOSE! NO WOMAN COULD EVER REPLACE ME! CARVING MENHIRS IS FAR TOO DELICATE A JOB!

CHIEF VITALSTATISTIX! CACOFONIX IS PLANNING TO LEAVE US OVER A WOMAN BARD!

YOU MEAN HE'S IN LOVE?

NO, BUT HE'S ALL UPSET TO THINK HE'S BEING REPLACED BY A WOMAN FROM OUT-SIDE THE VILLAGE!

OH, I HAVE EVERY FAITH IN US! WE'LL SEE THIS WOMAN BARD OFF IN DOUBLE-QUICK TIME!

MEANWHILE WE MUST PERSUADE CACOFONIX TO STAY. HE'S EXCELLENT COMPANY WHEN HE DOESN'T SING!

THE WHOLE VILLAGE ASKS YOU NOT TO LEAVE, CACOFONIX!

FAREWELL, YOU UNGRATEFUL LOT! QUALIS ARTIFEX PEREO!*

*WHAT AN ARTIST PERISHES WITH ME! (LATIN SAYING WRONGLY ATTRIBUTED TO NERO)

3A

LOOK...JUST TO SHOW HOW FOND WE ARE OF YOU, WE'RE EVEN WILLING TO... TO LET YOU SING!

OH NO, YOU WON'T GET ME TO SING! OH NO, YOU WON'T GET ME TO SING!!!

BONG! BONG! BONG!

WHERE ARE YOU GOING, CACOFO-NIX?

I AM RETIRING TO MY LITTLE PIED-À-L'AIR* IN THE HEART OF THE FOREST TO MEDITATE ON MAN'S INGRATITUDE!

* A BARD'S SECOND HOME.

IT'S SAD TO SEE OUR BARD LEAVE THE VILLAGE!

YES, THOUGH IT'S NOT ALWAYS THE BEST WHO ARE TAKEN!

IS THIS THE VILLAGE OF LOONIES?

!?

3B

LOOKS LIKE IT'S NOT ALWAYS THE BEST WHO REPLACE THEM, EITHER!

PFFFFFF!

SSSH!

MADAM, I AM THE CHIEFTAIN OF THIS VILLAGE! KINDLY MODERATE YOUR LANGUAGE!

SORRY, BUT THAT'S HOW THEY'VE BEEN DESCRIBING YOUR OPPIDUM IN EVERY MANSIO* WHERE I ASKED THE WAY SINCE LUTETIA!

*KIND OF MOTEL ON THE ROMAN ROADS.

PFFFFFHEE! HEEHEE!

SHUT UP, OBELIX!

SO YOU'RE THE... WHAT DO WE CALL YOU? BARDESS? BARDETTE?

JUST BARD! MY NAME IS BRAVURA, AND TELL YOUR HYSTERICAL FRIEND TO STOP THAT SILLY GIGGLING OR I SHALL LOSE MY TEMPER!

HOHOHAHAHA!

ER...PLEASE FORGIVE MY FRIEND! HE'S NEVER SEEN A WOMAN WEARING THE BREECHES BEFORE!

YOU IGNORANT RUSTICS! ORIENTAL 'DJEANS', LEVIX AND LEGGINGS LIKE THESE ARE ALL THE RAGE IN LUTETIA!

SRRR!

IT ISN'T THAT... TEEHEEHEE! EVERYONE KNOWS IT'S VERTICAL STRIPES THAT ARE SLIMMING... HO! HO! HO!

!

RIGHT, FATSO, LET'S SEE IF YOU'RE AS STRONG ON MATHEMATICS AS AESTHETICS! SAY YOUR III TIMES TABLE!

EASY! ONE TIMES THREE IS ASTERIX, DOGMATIX AND ME, BUT THREE TIMES BOARS MAKES A LOT MORE ON THE TABLE, OF COURSE!

RIGHT. I WANT TO SEE YOU AND YOUR STRIPES IN MY CLASS TOMORROW, GET IT?

?!

BONG! BONG! BONG!

BUT I CAN'T! NOT TOMORROW! I'VE GOT MENHIRS TO DELIVER!

OBELIX, PLEASE! DON'T COMPLICATE MATTERS!

PFFFFFF TEEHEEHEE!

WE'VE BEEN LOOKING FORWARD TO SEEING YOU, MA'AM! I'M IMPEDIMENTA, THE CHIEF'S WIFE. MEET MRS UNHYGIENIX, MRS FULLIAUTOMATIX AND MRS GERIATRIX.

JUST CALL ME BRAVURA!

WE'RE HAVING A LITTLE PARTY IN YOUR HONOUR THIS EVENING, TO INTRODUCE OUR NEW BARD TO THE VILLAGERS.

YOU MAY FIND THEM A BIT RUSTIC, BUT THEY'RE FULL OF FUN!

SO I'VE SEEN! WELL, WHERE'S MY OFFICIAL RESIDENCE?

YOUR OFFICIAL RES... OH, YES, OF COURSE!

WHY NOT USE CACOFONIX'S HUT? HE LEFT... HE DIDN'T KNOW THE SCORE.

YES, HE GOT THE WIND UP!

SO IT'S YOURS!

NO STRINGS ATTACHED! COME ALONG... YOU MUST BE WORN OUT, WALKING ALL THIS WAY!

I DON'T HITCH LIFTS. YOU NEVER KNOW WHAT MALE CHAUVINIST PIG YOU MAY MEET!

OINK?

54

THERE! RATHER HIGH UP, BUT THE AIR IS VERY PURE!

HUMPH! NOT BAD!

SOON AFTER-WARDS...

YOU KNOW ME, ASTERIX: I'M NOT A MISOGYNIST, I'M NOT XENOPHOBIC, BUT I DON'T LIKE THAT FOREIGN WOMAN. SOMETHING TELLS ME SHE'S GOING TO BRING THE SKY DOWN ON OUR HEADS!

IT'S A LONG TIME SINCE ANYONE SWEPT UP AROUND HERE!

?!

WHAT DID I TELL YOU?

I KNEW CACOFONIX DIDN'T COMPOSE LIGHT MUSIC, BUT I HAD NO IDEA HE WAS A MAN OF SO MUCH NOTE!

TING!

5B

A PARTY IN HONOUR OF THAT ...THAT BARD! *HUMPH!* HONESTLY!

OH, I SEE! JUST FOR ONCE WE WELCOME A PERSON OF QUALITY AND EDUCATION TO THE VILLAGE, AND MISTER VITALSTATISTIX DOESN'T LIKE IT!

I DARE SAY HE'D PREFER THE BORING COMPANY OF THOSE COARSE, UNCULTIVATED BOORS WHO CHOSE HIM AS CHIEF!

LISTEN, 'PEDIMENTA DEAR...

AND STOP CALLING ME 'PEDIMENTA! IT'S COMMON! AND RIDICULOUS!

WHERE'S YOUR SHIELD OF OFFICE?

ONE OF MY SHIELD-BEARERS HAS LET ME DOWN, TIRED OUT, AND THE OTHER FLATLY REFUSES TO CARRY ME ALONE!

I THINK I NEED A SPARE SHIELD-BEARER!

YOU DO. THAT SHIELD IS ALWAYS BREAKING DOWN AT THE CRUCIAL MOMENT.

I DIDN'T THINK THERE COULD BE WOMEN BARDS!

WE ARE ENTERING THE MODERN ERA OF THE ANCIENT WORLD, ASTERIX, WHEN ANYTHING MAY HAPPEN!

SO IT'S ONLY RIGHT FOR A WOMAN TO BE CONSIDERED THE EQUAL OF A MAN, WITH ALL THE ASPIRATIONS AND AMBITIONS HITHERTO DENIED HER!

YOU MEAN THERE COULD BE WOMEN DRUIDS TOO?

OH, COME ON, ASTERIX, BE SERIOUS!

DO TELL US ABOUT GAY LUTETIA, DEAR BRAVURA! I HEAR IT'S BECOMING A GREAT CITY!

YES, IT'S REALLY CAPITAL!

WHAT ARE THE SUMMER FASHIONS THIS YEAR?

DO YOU THINK ORIENTAL DJEANS OR LEGGINGS WOULD FLATTER MY FIGURE?

WELCOME TO OUR NEW B

NIGHT BRINGS THE VILLAGE PEACE AND CALM...

...BROKEN ONLY BY THE SNORING OF THE VILLAGE COCKEREL, WHOSE ADENOIDS ARE STILL GIVING HIM TROUBLE.

RRRRRRR! ZZZZ!

IN LUTETIA'S FAIR CITY, WHERE GIRLS ARE SO PRETTY...

BOOM! BOOM!

COCK-A-WHATSIT?

...I FIRST SET MY EYES...

BOOM! BOOM!

...ON SWEET MOLLIA MALONUS...

...AS SHE WHEELED HER WHEELBARROW...

BOOM! BOOM!

COCK-A-DOODLE-DOO!

AND YOU CALL THAT A PERSON OF QUALITY AND EDUCATION?!

SO? BARDS DON'T CLOCK-WATCH!

8A

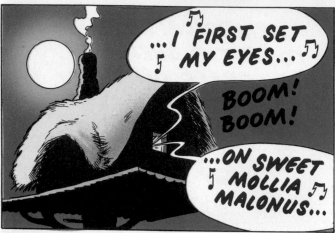

...THROUGH STREETS BROAD AND NARROW...

BOOM! BOOM!

MUCH THE SAME AS CACOFONIX, EXCEPT IT ISN'T RAINING!

...CRYING CARDIA AND MYTILI...

BOOM! BOOM!

CHOP! CHOP!

...ALIVE-ALIVE-OOOOOOOH!

CRAASH!

SHE WAS REALLY GETTING ME DOWN!

GETTING *YOU* DOWN? MALE CHAUVINIST BOAR!

WOOOOAAHH!

DON'T CRY, DOGMATIX! I'LL ASK GETAFIX TO MAKE THE TREE GROW AGAIN TOMORROW!

8B

AT THIS VERY MOMENT, IN ROME...

WELL, MANLIUS CLAPHAMOMNIBUS, HOW ARE YOU DOING WITH THAT 'VERY SPECIAL CENTURY' YOU WERE GOING TO RECRUIT?

IT'S READY TO GO, O CAESAR! YOUR NEW SECRET WEAPON MERELY AWAITS YOUR ORDERS TO EMBARK!

I DON'T WANT ANY WITNESSES TO THIS BUSINESS, UNDERSTAND? *NO WITNESSES!*

EVERY PRECAUTION SHALL BE TAKEN, O CAESAR, I SWEAR IT!

IF THE EXISTENCE OF YOUR CENTURY BECAME KNOWN, I SHOULD BE VULNERABLE TO MY ENEMIES IN THE SENATE AND THE LAUGHING-STOCK OF ROME! SO WATCH IT, CLAPHAMOMNIBUS!

GULP!

AND THUS A ROMAN SHIP, CARRYING CAESAR'S MYSTERIOUS SECRET WEAPON, SETS SAIL IN THE DIRECTION OF... *GAUL!*

POOR OBELIX! WHAT A PITY HE COULDN'T COME ON THIS HUNT...

... HE'D HAVE HAD SUCH FUN!

GLUG! GLUG! GLUG!

A LITTLE LATER, IN THE FORTIFIED CAMP OF AQUARIUM...

BY JUPITER! ANY-ONE WOULD THINK ALL GAUL HAD BEEN TRAMPLING OVER YOU!

IT FEEL LIKE IT, FENTURION!

WE BUMPED INTO A BOAR...

...AND THAT LITTLE STINKER FROM THE VILLAGE OF INDOMITABLE GAULS!

GLORIA VICTIS!

BEAR UP, BOYS! ROME HAS PROMISED TO SEND OUR RELIEF SOON!

I FEAR VITALSTATISTIX MAY BE RIGHT. I'M AFRAID THIS BRAVURA WILL SOW DISCORD AMONG US!

NOW, NOW, LET'S NOT JUDGE HASTILY, ASTERIX!

AND FROM NOW ON YOU CAN SELL YOUR ROTTEN FISH BY YOURSELF!

FISHMONGER UNHYGIENIX

PAF!

OUCH!

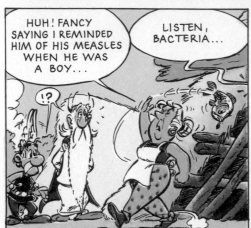

HUH! FANCY SAYING I REMINDED HIM OF HIS MEASLES WHEN HE WAS A BOY...

LISTEN, BACTERIA...

!?

BUT WHAT AM I GOING TO DO WITHOUT MY BREECHES?

THE DISHES, GERIATRIX DEAR! THE DISHES!

!!!

WAAAH! DON'T WANT TO LOOK LIKE THE NASTY BOYS!!!

GNNNN!

YOU'RE AS REACTIONARY AS YOUR FATHER!

WHAT DID I SAY JUST NOW?

LET'S GO AND DISCUSS THIS WITH VITALSTATISTIX!

BONG! BONG! BONG!

NO, 'PEDI... IMPEDIMENTA! NOT MY SHIELD!

YOUR SHIELD IS MY SHIELD!

SO THIS IS WOMAN'S PLACE IN GAULISH SOCIETY TODAY!

!

YOU MAY BE WEARING THE BREECHES, BUT YOU NEEDN'T THINK YOU CAN EMULATE OUR PROUD MASCULINE BEARING!

THE VILLAGE COUNCIL MEETS...

WE MUST GO AND TELL THAT BARD SHE'S REDUNDANT BEFORE THINGS GET ANY WORSE. SHE MUST LEAVE THE VILLAGE.

I CAN THINK OF ONLY ONE WARRIOR PROUD AND BRAVE ENOUGH TO BREAK THAT NEWS!

WHO?

YOU, ASTERIX!

OH NO! WHY DOES IT HAVE TO BE ME? I'M NO PROUDER OR BRAVER THAN THE NEXT MAN, AND I'M REALLY NOT CUT OUT FOR THIS SORT OF...

ASTERIX, PLEASE! DON'T COMPLICATE MATTERS!

...MISSION!

PFFFFFFFFF!

PFFFFFFF!

BE FIRM AND UNYIELDING, ASTERIX!

WHERE ARE YOU GOING, ASTERIX?

GUESS!

WHY DID IT HAVE TO BE ME? I MEAN, I'M A BACHELOR! NONE OF THIS HAS ANYTHING TO DO WITH ME!

SOMETIMES I REALLY ENVY CACOFONIX, LIVING IN THE DEPTHS OF THE FOREST! (SIGH...)

SCHOOL

MA'AM... ER... I'VE BEEN SENT TO TELL YOU THAT...

AH, YOU'RE THE LITTLE FELLOW WHO ISN'T AFRAID OF THE BIG BOYS?

SCHOO

YOU KNOW, I LIKE YOU! I WANTED A WORD WITH YOU MYSELF!

SLAP!

TONIGHT GAULISH WOMEN'S MOVEMENT WORKSHOP *

WELL, BRAVURA, DO YOU LIKE IT HERE?

YES AND NO!

OH? WHAT DON'T YOU LIKE?

WELL, LOOK AT YOURSELF! YOU'RE THE FIRST LADY OF THIS VILLAGE, AND YOU SIT THERE DOING EMBROIDERY INSTEAD OF TAKING THE DESTINY OF YOUR PEOPLE IN HAND!

BUT...BUT VITALSTATISTIX IS...

FIDDLESTICKS! WHO BUT YOU KNOWS WHAT THE GAULISH WOMAN REALLY WANTS? NOT THAT SUPERANNUATED BORE!

WHAT'S THAT? SUPPER? MARINATED BOAR?

HUH! I'M OFF!

WAIT A MINUTE, BRAVURA...

NOW I WONDER WHO'S COOKED A GREAT BIG BOAR FOR HER DEAR LITTLE PIGGYWIGGY?

I AM NOT YOUR SLAVE!!!

16ª

COME INDOORS! I HAVE SOMETHING TO SAY TO YOU

HELP! WHAT HAVE I GONE AND DONE THIS TIME?

SO THAT'S IT! FROM NOW I SHALL SIT ON THE VILLAGE COUNCIL TOO. I'M THE CHIEF'S WIFE, RIGHT?

RIGHT! AND I'M THE CHIEF AROUND HERE!

OH YES?

OH YES!

PAF!

OKAY THEN, I'M LEAVING THE VILLAGE!!

LOOKS LIKE IMPEDIMENTA HIT THE ROOF!

AND THAT'S NOT ALL SHE HIT!

16ᵇ

WE'RE GOING TO TAKE A FREE VOTE ON WHETHER IMPEDIMENTA OR VITALSTATISTIX IS TO BE OUR CHIEF!

EACH IN TURN, WE SHALL ENTER MY HUT AND PLACE A PEBBLE IN THIS CASK TO INDICATE OUR CHOICE: WHITE PEBBLES FOR IMPEDIMENTA, YELLOW PEBBLES FOR VITALSTATISTIX.

OH, WHY MAKE IT SO COMPLICATED WHEN A SIMPLE SHOW OF HANDS WOULD DO?

SHE'S RIGHT! LET'S HAVE A SHOW OF HANDS!

HUH! WHY NOT A SHOW OF FEET WHILE WE'RE ABOUT IT?

OH YES, YOU'D GET A BIG KICK OUT OF THAT!

NOT EXACTLY UNANIMOUS, ARE THEY?

IT'S PERFECTLY SIMPLE! LET'S VOTE BY A SHOW OF HANDS TO SHOW IF WE WANT TO VOTE BY A SHOW OF HANDS!

ALL WHO WANT TO VOTE BY A SHOW OF HANDS SHOW THEIR HANDS!

RIGHT. ALL WHO DON'T WANT TO VOTE BY A SHOW OF HANDS SHOW THEIR HANDS!

ASTERIX, I DON'T QUITE UNDERSTAND THIS SHOW OF HANDS BUSINESS!

I DO! I CALL IT A POOR SHOW, AND I'M THROWING IN MY HAND!

BRAVURA GAVE ME A BLACK LOOK!

THIS IS TERRIBLE, OBELIX! I STRUCK A WOMAN!

THAT CERTAINLY CAN'T BE AS MUCH FUN AS THUMPING A ROMAN!

I'M SO ASHAMED! WHATEVER CAME OVER ME?

HEY... BETWEEN US, IT WOULDN'T HAVE COME OVER YOU WITH THE LOVELY PANACEA*, EH? TEEHEEHEE!

OBELIX, YOU'RE BEING SILLY!

ASTERIX!

*SEE ASTERIX THE LEGIONARY

IMPEDIMENTA HAS SUMMONED YOU TO APPEAR BEFORE THE VILLAGE COUNCIL THIS VERY DAY TO ANSWER CHARGES BROUGHT BY BRAVURA!

?!

I'VE A FEELING I SHALL SOON HAVE TO LEAVE THE VILLAGE MYSELF!

I WILL PERSONALLY UNDERTAKE YOUR DEFENCE AGAINST THIS DANGEROUS AND UNPRINCIPLED NEW BARD! TRUST ME, ASTERIX!

ASTERIX, YOU HAVE BROKEN OUR LAWS BY MALTREATING OUR GUEST! YOU HAVE BROUGHT GAULISH GALLANTRY INTO DISREPUTE! WE THEREFORE SENTENCE YOU TO TEMPORARY EXILE FROM THE VILLAGE, TO MEDITATE ON THE CONSEQUENCES OF YOUR ACTION!

OH, MARVELLOUS! SO THE PERSON WHO'S DESTROYED THE HARMONY OF OUR VILLAGE IS ON THE COUNCIL, WHILE THE HERO WHO HAS DONE SO MUCH TO SAFEGUARD OUR LIBERTIES IS BANISHED! BRILLIANT!

WHO NEEDS HEROES? IT WOULD BE MORE SENSIBLE TO EXTEND THE HAND OF FRIENDSHIP TO THE LEGIONS WHO SO GENEROUSLY OFFER US THE BENEFITS OF THE PAX ROMANA!

SO WHO NEEDS YOUR ADVICE, YOU VIPER???

AND WHO NEEDS YOUR CAULDRON, YOU DECREPIT OLD OWL?

VERY WELL! IN THE CIRCUMSTANCES...

I'M LEAVING THE VILLAGE!!!

!

MEANWHILE, ON THE COAST NEAR THE FORTIFIED CAMP OF AQUARIUM...

STAND BY TO DISEMBARK!

CREEEEAK!

OH FOR SOME NICE SEA AIR!

I'LL ASK YOU TO BE PATIENT A LITTLE LONGER. DON'T COME OUT BEFORE I GIVE THE ORDER!

AND IN THE FORTIFIED CAMP OF AQUARIUM...

SNIFF! THE GAULS HAB GOT A FORBIDABLE ABD DABGEROUS WEAPOB...

?!

BLOW!

...THEIR WRETCHEB BARB WHO CAB OBLY SING SO BADLY...

...THAT HE BRINGS DOWB THE CURSE OF THE GOBS WHEBEVER HE SINGS!

QUOB ERAT BEMONSTRAN-BAAA... TISHOOO!

IT'LL BE A GREAT RELIEF WHEN THE RELIEF GETS HERE!

THE RELIEF'S HERE, CENTURION!

229

ARE...ARE YOU THE RELIEF?

SO TO SPEAK! MY ORDERS FROM CAESAR ARE TO TELL YOU TO LEAVE CAMP BEFORE THE RELIEF RELIEVES YOU!

AND SUPPOSE I REFUSE TO LEAVE CAMP BEFORE THE RELIEF RELIEVES US?

THEN YOU'LL BE RELIEVED OF YOUR DUTIES AND GO TO RELIEVE THE MONOTONY OF THE DIET OF THE LIONS IN THE CIRCUS!

WE'RE LEAVING CAMP!

MEANWHILE, IN THE FOREST SEPARATING THE VILLAGE FROM THE ROMAN CAMP...

WE'RE NOT TOO BADLY OFF HERE WHILE WE WAIT FOR OUR GOOD LADIES TO SEE SENSE!

BUT WE MUST BE ON OUR GUARD, IN CASE THE ROMANS TAKE THEIR CHANCE TO SEIZE THE VILLAGE!

OBELIX AND I WILL GO AND KEEP WATCH ON THEM!

228

STOP IT! STOP IT AT ONCE!

PIF! PAF!

A FINE PERFORMANCE BY THE ROMAN ARMY, EH? YOU DON'T EVEN NEED GAULS TO FIGHT NOW! HOW THEY'D LAUGH IF THEY COULD SEE YOU!

I DON'T SEE ANYTHING TO LAUGH ABOUT!

SSH, OBELIX!

I THOUGHT I TOLD YOU TO LEAVE CAMP, CENTURION!

LISTEN, WHAT EXACTLY IS THE IDEA?

COME HERE A MINUTE! I HAVE SOMETHING TO TELL YOU!

?

25A

I GOT THE IDEA OF RECRUITING THIS CENTURY OF WOMEN TO CONQUER THE GAULS AND OCCUPY THEIR VILLAGE AT LONG LAST!

YOU THINK YOUR SECRET WEAPON WILL SUCCEED WHERE WE'VE FAILED, DO YOU?

?!?

THEIR FAMOUS GAULISH GALLANTRY WILL PREVENT THE INDOMITABLE VILLAGERS FROM FIGHTING WOMEN, EVEN WOMEN IN UNIFORM!

I GET IT! RIGHT, WE'LL LEAVE CAMP!

OH NO, YOU WON'T! NOW YOU KNOW THE SECRET YOU'RE ALL CONFINED TO BARRACKS!

?!?

QUICK! WE MUST GO AND WARN OUR CHIEF!

ASTERIX, WHAT'S GAULISH GALLANTRY?

25B

BY TOUTATITH, THETHE ROMANTH ARE CRATHY!

HERE, SONNY! WHERE ARE ALL THE VILLAGE WOMEN?

CLING! CLANG!

THEY'RE ALL AT THCOOL! UTH CHILDREN AREN'T HAVING LETHONTH ANY MORE! IT'TH GREAT!

?

LET'S TAKE A LOOK, OBELIX!

SCHOOL

CLAP! CLAP! CLAP!

BRAVO!

AND STILL IN THE DIORIX COLLECTION, AFTER THE MENHIR ROSE OUTFIT, WE PRESENT THE DREAMY DOLMEN EVENING DRESS!

CLAP! CLAP! CLAP! CLAP! CLAP! CLAP! CLAP! CLAP!

THIS IS REALLY WEIRD!

SNIFF! SNIFF! SNIFF! YOU'RE RIGHT... I CAN'T SMELL UNHYGIENIX'S UNFRESH FISH ANY MORE!

CLAP! CLAP! CLAP!

HEY... WHAT'S GOING ON?

BRAVURA HAS BROUGHT SOME FAMOUS FASHION DESIGNERS FROM LUTETIA TO PRESENT THEIR SPRING COLLECTIONS!

CLAP! CLAP! CLAP!

IT'S... IT'S ASTERIX!

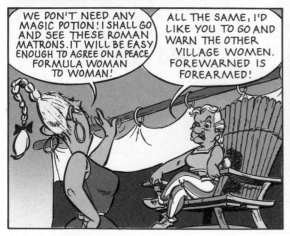

32

HOW'S MY PIGGY-WIGGY, ASTERIX? I DO HOPE HE HASN'T CAUGHT COLD!

!!!

IT'S SO DAMP IN THE FOREST AT THIS TIME OF YEAR. TAKE HIM THESE WARM CLOTHES!

AND REMIND HIM THAT IF HE OVEREATS HE'S LIABLE TO GET AN ATTACK OF THE GOUT!

FISHMONG UNH

HERE, ASTERIX!

?

TELL UNHYGIENIX TO TO WRAP UP WELL! NIGHTS ARE CHILLY IN THE FOREST!

FOR FULLIAUTOMATIX! I KNOW THAT GREAT LOUT ...HE CATCHES COLD AT THE DROP OF A HELMET!

29ª

FOR GERIATRIX, TO KEEP HIS RHEUMATICS AWAY!

AND THESE TO KEEP HIS HAND IN!

?

!

I WANT TO ASK YOU A FAVOUR, ASTERIX!

HEY, ASTERIX!

HEY, OBELIX!

OBELIX!

YOOHOO, ASTERIX!

SOON AFTERWARDS...

WELL, ASTERIX, WHAT NEWS HAVE YOU BROUGHT BACK FROM THE VILLAGE?

NOT MUCH NEWS...

...BUT NO END OF ADVICE!

?!!

29ᵇ

33

THE CENTURY OF WOMEN HAS PITCHED TEMPORARY CAMP NEAR THE FORTIFIED CAMP OF AQUARIUM, IN LINE WITH THE REGULATIONS...

...SLIGHTLY MODIFIED HERE AND THERE!

JUST WHAT IS THIS?

THIS PRINT? IT'S A FAST DYE: GUARANTEED NOT TO RUN IN THE WASH!

SOME OF THE DISGRUNTLED MEN CONFINED TO BARRACKS NEXT DOOR RELIEVE THEIR FEELINGS ABOUT THEIR RELIEF.

IF WOMEN CAN JOIN THE LEGIONS NOW, WHAT USE ARE WE GOING TO BE?

I COULD TELL YOU! I WOULDN'T EVEN MIND BEING A *DOMESTICUS** OVER IN THAT CAMP!

*SERVANT

MEANWHILE...

BRAVURA! SHE MUST BE GOING TO THE ROMAN CAMP! LET'S FOLLOW HER DISCREETLY!

HALT, GAUL!

YOU'RE A WOMAN TOO! THAT MAKES US SISTERS, SO LET'S SHAKES HANDS, ROMAN!

TCHAC!

34

THAT ROMAN SISTER ISN'T VERY GALLANT!

YOU SAID IT!

WHAT BRINGS YOU HERE, GAULISH WOMAN?

I'VE COME TO OFFER PEACE BETWEEN ROME AND THE VILLAGE OF INDOMITABLE GAULS, AND THIS IS THE WELCOME I GET!

TEEHEEHEE! SO THE INDOMITABLE GAULS ARE SURRENDERING! I WOULDN'T HAVE THOUGHT IT WOULD BE SO QUICK AND EASY!

IT'S NOT THE INDOMITABLE GAULS SURRENDERING. IT'S THEIR WOMEN WHO WANT PEACE!

OH YES?

I WANT NO TRUCK WITH YOUR PEACE PROPOSALS, WOMAN! THE VILLAGE WILL BE DESTROYED, AND ITS PEOPLE WILL END THEIR DAYS IN CHAINS IN THE TULLIANUM*!

*PRISON IN ROME WHERE VERCINGETORIX AMONG OTHERS WAS INCARCERATED. 314

SMACK!

YOU'RE NOTHING BUT A LOT OF BARBARIANS!

ALL OF A SUDDEN I LIKE OUR NEW BARD BETTER!

I WANT A WORD WITH BRAVURA. SEE YOU LATER, OBELIX!

OH? RIGHT!

CONGRATULATIONS ON YOUR COURAGE, BRAVURA!

HUH! JUST A SET OF OAFS! THEY'RE BENEATH OUR CONTEMPT!

YOU KNOW YOUR WAY ROUND LUTETIA, RIGHT?

I DO. WHY DO YOU ASK?

BECAUSE THIS TIME IT'S MY TURN TO MAKE YOU A PROPOSITION!

!

318

WE'RE AGREED, THEN, BRAVURA?

ABSOLUTELY AGREED, ASTERIX!

DONE IT! I'VE MADE MY PEACE WITH BRAVURA!

TEEHEE! SO I HEAR!

THERE GOES ANOTHER BACHELOR!

IT WAS BOUND TO HAPPEN SOME DAY!

AH, THE JOYS OF LOVE!

32[9]

WHAT ARE ALL THESE SNIDE REMARKS IN AID OF?

TEE-HEEHEE!

HO, HO, HO!

YOU'VE BEEN TELLING THEM A LOAD OF NONSENSE, RIGHT?

WELL...ER...NO! YES, WELL...

I MEAN, IT'S NOTHING TO BE ASHAMED OF, ASTERIX...

OH, REALLY, YOU'RE ALL IDIOTS! I'M NOT GOING TO TELL YOU THE PLAN I'VE COOKED UP WITH BRAVURA, SO THERE!

THUD!

MEANWHILE, IN THE WOMEN LEGIONARIES' CAMP...

WELL, CENTURION, WHAT'S YOUR PLAN FOR OCCUPYING THE VILLAGE?

EASY! I BARGE IN AND I OCCUPY IT! BUT I'LL SEND A PATROL FIRST, TO BE ON THE SAFE SIDE. YOU NEVER KNOW!

YOU'RE TO GO THROUGH THE FOREST AND APPROACH THE GAULISH VILLAGE. COME BACK AND REPORT ALL YOU SEE. DISMISS!

32[B]

IT STARTED WITH A HORRIBLE HOWL...

...FOLLOWED BY A DOWNPOUR WHICH BROUGHT OUT SNAKES AND SPIDERS...

...AND EVEN WOLVES!

I'M SURE THERE'S A DRAGON IN THAT FOREST!

STOP BEING SUCH DRIPS, WILL YOU?

REGULAR AS CLOCKWORK, AS PATROL FOLLOWS PATROL...

GNNAAAHHAHOOOUURR

...DOWNPOUR FOLLOWS DOWNPOUR...

RRIIIIIIIIOUOUUU

① OWL SWEAR-WORDS

...AND DAY FOLLOWS MISERABLE DAY...

I CAN'T SEE WHY A FEW DROPS OF RAIN AND A HOWL OR SO SHOULD...

NO, WELL, YOU'RE NOT THE ONE FACING THE MUSIC, CLAPHAM-OMNIBUS!

...IN BOTH CAMPS.

THAT WAS THE LAST BOAR IN THE FOREST, AND I CAN'T EVEN COOK IT!

BLOW!

NOW, ASTERIX, ARE YOU GOING TO TELL US WHY THIS SUDDEN ENTHUSIASM FOR CACOFONIX'S SINGING?

IT'S GIVEN ME THE TIME I NEEDED TO SET UP MY PLAN!

BUT WHAT IS THIS PLAN OF YOURS?

YES, WHAT EXACTLY IS IT?

TRUST ME A LITTLE LONGER! ALL I ASK IS FOR YOU TO WAIT FOR ME NEAR THE VILLAGE, KEEPING UNDER COVER. WHATEVER HAPPENS, DON'T INTERVENE!

OBELIX AND I STILL HAVE A FEW THINGS TO DO. COMING, OBELIX?

?!

CHAAARGE!

WHEEEEEEEEEEEEEEEEEEEEEEEEEEEEEEEEEEEEEEEEE

40

41

A LITTLE LATER...

I'M SORRY, CACOFONIX, BUT YOUR VOICE MIGHT CURDLE THE MAGIC POTION!

GLUG! GLUG!

HUH!

VILLAGERS! PROUD AND NOBLE WARRIORS! ONCE AGAIN WE FIND OURSELVES OBLIGED TO CONFRONT OUR MORTAL ENEMY! THE ANXIOUS GAZE OF THE FREE AND ANCIENT WORLD IS TURNED UPON YOUR POWERFUL BREASTS, READY TO FEND OFF THE HEGEMONY OF A DICTATORSHIP WHICH WILL GO SO FAR AS TO ATTACK WOMEN...

...AND CHILDREN!

THE GOOD POTION GUIDE SHOULD GIVE TODAY'S BREW SEVERAL STARS!

YES, AND THE ROMANS WILL SOON BE SEEING PLENTY!

CAEFAR WILL BE FURIOUF, THAT'F FOR FURE! LUCKILY I CAN FTILL CALL ON THE OTHER FORTIFIED ROMAN CAMPF!

AND IN THE CAMP OF TOTORUM...

YOU LOOK RATHER RUFFLED, PATRICIAN! LIKE A DRINK?

YEF, PLEAFE! WITH A FTRAW IF POFFIBLE!

WELL, WELL! SO THE COWARDLY GAULS HAVE ABANDONED THEIR VILLAGE, LEAVING ONLY WOMEN AND CHILDREN TO GUARD IT!

JUFT AF I FAID, FENTURION! SLUP!

RAISE THE ALARM! THE GAULS ARE ATTACKING.!!!

?!

CHARGE, BOYS!

LEAVE THEM TO ME! LEAVE THEM TO ME!

DON'T BE SELFISH, OBELIX!

45

HERE, PIGGYWIGGY! THE SHIELD SUITS YOU BETTER THAN ME!

YOU KNOW YOU CAN USE IT WHENEVER YOU LIKE, 'PEDI... 'PEDIMENTA!

NO HARD FEELINGS, BRAVURA?

NO HARD FEELINGS, ASTERIX!

ALL'S WELL THAT ENDS WELL. A CERTAIN CHEERFULNESS EVEN SEEMS TO HAVE CREPT INTO ROME... OR MOST OF IT!

THERE'S A STRANGE SENSE OF GAIETY IN ROME, O CAESAR!

SHUT UP, IDIOT, AND PACK MY BAGS! I'M GOING AWAY TO MY COUNTRY PALACE FOR A WHILE!

HA! HA! HA! HEE! HEE! HEE! HO! HO! HO! HEE! HEE! HO! HO! HO! HA! HA! HA! HO! HO! HO! HEE! HEE! HEE! HA! HA! HO! HO! HO!

AND FINALLY, IN HAPPY CELEBRATION OF THE RETURN OF DOMESTIC PEACE AND GENERAL GOODWILL, THE TRADITIONAL BANQUET IS HELD IN THE MIDDLE OF THE VILLAGE. BRAVURA AND ALL THE GAULISH WOMEN ARE GUESTS OF HONOUR. EVEN CACOFONIX IS INVITED... ON CERTAIN CONDITIONS.

DO YOU LIKE IT IN OUR VILLAGE, BRAVURA?

YES, BUT I MUST GET BACK TO LUTETIA SOON! AND BY WAY OF APOLOGY I'VE PROMISED TO TAKE YOUR BARD BACK WITH ME AND INTRODUCE HIM TO ZIEGFELDFOLLIX, THE GREAT LUTETIAN IMPRESARIO!

FRIENDS, GAULS, COUNTRY-MEN! IT IS WITH DEEP EMOTION THAT...

SCRUNCH! SCRUNCH!

I JUTHT CAN'T WAIT TO BE GROWN UP AND HAVE FUN!

ME TOO! THEN I'LL BE YOUR CHIEF!

The End

- UDERZO - 91

48

PRINTED IN BELGIUM BY proost INTERNATIONAL BOOK PRODUCTION